# Heard in the Cougait

Poems by Donald Campbell
From the engravings of Walter Geikie

# Donald Campbell

Born in Caithness in 1940, Donald Campbell grew up in Edinburgh where he still lives. A full-time writer since 1974, he is active as playwright, theatre historian, stage director, script writer and poet. He is an Honorary Fellow of the Association of Scottish Literary Studies and a Life Member of the Writers' Guild of Great Britain.

# Heard in the cougait

Poems by Donald Campbell

From the engravings of Walter Geikie

GRACE NOTE PUBLICATIONS

Heard in the Cougait
This edition published 2017 by
Grace Note Publications C.I.C.
Grange of Locherlour,
Ochtertyre, PH7 4JS,
Scotland

books@gracenotereading.co.uk
www.gracenotepublications.co.uk

ISBN 978-1-907676-92-5

Copyright © Donald Campbell 2017

Four of the poems – *Faither's fou, Mr. and Mrs. Anderson, Soutar Johnnie* and *The Jolly Beggars* appeared without images in Fras18, edited by Walter Perrie, Fras Publications

A catalogue record for this book is available from the British Library

# Introduction

Walter Geikie R.S.A. (1795-1837) was born in Drummond Street, South Edinburgh in the November of 1795. Unfortunately, when he was still a babe, he contracted a fever which robbed him of his hearing and as a result he never developed the power of speech. This created some difficulty in the matter of his education and it was only because of the patience and persistence of his father that he eventually learned to read and write. Perhaps, however, his handicap played a part in developing his powers of observation. Certainly, he showed a high degree of artistic talent from an early age.

In 1809, at the age of just fourteen, he was accepted as a pupil by the landscape artist Patrick Gibson (1782-1835). Three years later, Geikie was admitted as a student to the Trustees Academy, forerunner of the Edinburgh College of Art, where he studied under a famous teacher of drawing, John Grahame. The first exhibition of his work took place in 1815 and he was appointed as an Associate of the Royal Scottish Academy in 1931, receiving a Fellowship three years later, in 1834.

Although he completed a few paintings, Geikie's main medium was pen and ink drawing and he earned his living by supplying etchings for book plates. He received his first commission in 1829 and continued drawing until his death in 1837. Four years later, a collected edition of his plates was published under the title *Etchings Illustrative of Scottish Character and Scenery*, with a biographical introduction by Sir Thomas Dick Lauder (John Stewart, Glasgow.1841).

When I first came across Geikie's prints I was immediately struck by their near photographic quality and by the fact that his characters are portrayed in specific situations, thereby providing us a detailed picture of working-class life in the Victorian era.

Donald Campbell<br>Edinburgh 2017

# Contents

| | |
|---|---|
| Introduction | 5 |
| Faither's Fou | 9 |
| Show Jamie | 11 |
| Mr. and Mrs. Anderson | 12 |
| Soutar Johnny | 13 |
| The Jolly Beggars | 14 |
| Hallow Fair | 16 |
| Come to Mammy, Dearie | 18 |
| He's had plenty! | 20 |
| Street Snab | 22 |
| Orphan Laddies | 24 |
| Blind Fiddler | 26 |
| Heard in the Cougait | 28 |
| Notes & Acknowledgment | 30 |

# Faither's Fou

*Very Fou*

Faither's fou; his wages spent
On countless cups of skichan ale
Dear knows where we'll find the rent!
My mither says he wants the jail!

On countless cups of skichan ale!
The silly sacket has nae shame
His appetites maun aye prevail
Then he'll come stottering, stotious, hame.

The silly sacket has nae shame
We're full up on the grocer's slate
when he comes stottering, stotious, hame.
What makes him aye sae profligate?

We're full up on the grocer's slate,
There's fient a farthing on his tail —
What makes him aye sae profligate?
His appetites maun aye prevail!

There's fient a farthing on his tail —
He'll no repay what he's been lent.
My mither says he wants the jail!
Dear knows how we will pay the rent!

He'll no repay what he's been lent.
His appetites maun aye prevail.
Faither's fou; his wages spent
On countless cups of skichan ale.

# Show Jamie

*Show Jamie*

Come on, Billy, let me see.
It's no like you to roar and greet
And raise a ruction in the street.
Ye needna be sae sweirt with me.

I'm your brother and I care;
Ye ken I'll fix ye up a treat.
So come awa and have a seat
And tell my why ye're feeling sair.

Mither and Faither baith agree
That I can best pull off the cure.
It's nothing but a smitch of stour!
*Oh come on, Billy! Let me see!*

# Mr. and Mrs. Anderson

Forty year syne, his brow was brent;
her manner somewhat diffident.
Black as the raven was his hair;
her face was free from lines of care.
Here at the foot of their auld stair,
their love's still warm and confident.

But such was aye their sole intent.
Thegither they would be content.
Thegither they would climb the hill
and here they are thegither still.
It takes a lifetime to fulfil
the marriage vows they made and meant.

No longer young and innocent,
she's still his lady, he's her gent.
The pair of them maun aye combine.
He's Harlequin, she's Columbine;
just as they were when first aquent
Forty year syne.

*The Auld Couple*

# Soutar Johnny

*Tam o' Shanter and Soutar Johnnie*

As Soutar Johnny supped his ale
he often would recount the tale
of the adventure that befell
his auld pal Tam ae market day.
It seems that Tam had met the deil
at Alloway.

Soutar told the tale in jest
and never knew and never guessed
that Robert Burns sat with the rest
and took a note
for *Tam O'Shanter*, quite the best
remembered poem he ever wrote.

# The Jolly Beggars

*The Jolly Beggars*

*Boozing and schmoozing, all night long
Everybody's singing the same old song.*

Here's an old soldier, coming on strong
*Boozing and schmoozing, all night long.*

The floozy by his side is doing no wrong
*Everybody's singing the same old song.*

Merry Andrew's happy, banging his gong
*Boozing and schmoozing, all night long*

Here comes the fiddler, limping along
*Everybody's singing the same old song.*

The kirk-bells ring out; ding, dang, and dong!
*Boozing and schmoozing, all night long.*

Little Danny Campbell, excited by the throng
*Sat down in a corner and wrote this song.*

# Hallow Fair

*Hallow Fair*

At summer's end, a certain chill
pervades Auld Reekie's air
as traders by the dozen fill
Grassmarket's sheltered square
While jugglers, clowns and fiddlers fill
the empty spaces there.
Wat, Tam and Tibbie, James and Jill,
dressed in their best, prepare
to dally and daff and have their fill
of sheer delight
when dancing at the Hallow Fair.

On luckenbooths you'll find displayed
delightful and delicious fare;
Corstorphine cream that's freshly made

and plenty gingerbread to spare!
Macaronies are on parade,
with lippies full of lemonade,
petticoats flouncing everywhere
so tunefully the music's played
both day and night
for dancing at the Hallow Fair,

Each chancer and each merry maid
is certainly aware
There's money in the equine trade
and look to take their share.
Such clever dicks
may get their licks
Meanwhile, we'd best beware
that crafty dips and three-card tricks
are like to bite
when dancing at the Hallow Fair.

As shelties canter up the causey
horse-copers place their bets
and sonsie quines, all jimp and gaucy,
skip deftly owre the sunlit setts,
Our laddies need have no regrets
to see so many mignonettes,
if they're inclined to stare.
There's no way that the mind forgets
the pleasing sight
of dancing at the Hallow Fair.

# Come to Mammy, Dearie

*Come to Mammy, dearie!*

Come to Mammy, dearie!
Tell me what's adae
Is it sair?
Tell me where
I'll soother it away.

Your brither's looking leerie.
What was that ye say?
He's no been kind?

Weill, never mind
I'll sort him right away!

Your faither's unco wearie
I canna think he'll stay.
It's such a shame
So let's gang hame
We'll come back another day.

*Come to Mammy, dearie!*
*Tell me what's adae*
*Is it sair?*
*Tell me where*
*I'll soother it away.*

# He's had plenty!

*He's just gotten plenty for the day*

When Singing Jimmy sang his song
in a voice so clear and strong
all his friends would sing along
— and he had plenty!

The sweet sound of that glorious voice
Would fairly gar the hairt rejoice
but he'd no listen to advice
— and he had plenty!

Let him have sixpence on his tail
The company he'd aye regale
They'd celebrate with pints of ale
and he had plenty!

Jamie Balfour was his name.
In Jenny Ha's he won his fame
But it's high time he headed hame
— for he's had plenty!

# Street Snab

*Cobler and Customer*

Kenspeckle on the street
Big Nellie his helpmeet,
The snab at his jack
maks shoon that fit folks' feet

He'll cut and sew and tack
Turn leather snod and swack
and let Big Nellie hawk the gear
she stores in her knapsack.

Gin onybody wants to speir
at fowk that gaither here
tae watch him at his work
ilkane o them wad volunteer
'A douce-like chiel ye maunna fear
— his name is William Burke.'

# Orphan Laddies

*Boiling Potatoes*

It's braw, it's braw, it's bully and braw;
as braw as braw can be.
Five cannier callants ye never saw
*than Sandy Nicol and Wullie McGraw,
Doddy and Davie and me.*

Five cannier callants ye never saw
Nor ever yet will see.
We hae nae Maw, we hae nae Paw

*just Sandy Nicol and Wullie McGraw,
Doddy and Davie and me.*

We hae nae Maw, we hae nae Paw
Orphaned laddies are we.
It's aa for ane and ane for aa
*That's Sandy Nicol and Wullie McGraw,
Doddy and Davie and me.*

It's aa for ane and ane for aa
And that's hou it maun be.
Life can whiles be reuch and raw
*for Sandy Nicol and Wullie McGraw,
Doddy and Davie and me.*

Life can whiles be reuch and raw
Whiles lichtsome and carefree.
and braw, sae braw, aye bully and braw;
It's aa for ane and ane for aa
We hae nae Maw, we hae nae Paw
Five cannier callants ye never saw
*nor Sandy Nicol and Wullie McGraw,
Doddy and Davie and me.*

# Blind Fiddler

*The Blind Fiddler*

He'll gang his ain gait, never let
his vision pass wi vanished sicht.
He sees nae mair nor cauld dark nicht
— but he's no done wi looking yet.

Orra fowk that strive and sweat
are eident aye tae see him richt.
His dancing fiddle, pure and bricht,
plays airs they never can forget.

Their pennies keep him free frae debt
and he lives better than he micht.
His cupboard's full, his shelter's ticht.
His life is as guid as it can get
— and he's no done wi living yet.

# Heard in the Cougait

*The Cowgate at the foot of Libberton Wynd*

Is it no a crying shame?
Johnnie Dowie's gane awa.
We've tint the howff that brocht him fame
Liberton Wynd is doomed anaa!

Johnnie Dowie's gane awa.
We gaither here to praise his name.
The doucest chiel we ever saw.
This auld toun will never be the same.

We've tint the howff that bore his name
Its ale was strang, its crack was braw,
its feeding fit tae please the wame.
Its douncome ane we ne'er foresaw.

Liberton Wynd is doomed anaa
As mony a faimly tines its hame
this ootcome makes nae sense ava.
Och! Is it no a crying shame?

# Notes & Acknowledgements

Most of these images appear in *The Etchings of Walter Geikie, R.S.A.* by Roy Morris (Print Collectors Quarterly, London 1935). The following three images appear here by permission of the Edinburgh Central Library's Capital Collections; *Hallow Fair, Come to Mammy, Dearie* and *He's just gotten plenty for the day*. Some 90 Geikie engravings can be found on the website <www.capitalcollections.org.uk>

*Faither's Fou* — Skichan Ale or Treacle Beer, a by-product of the brewing process, was very popular in Geikie's time. If it was very cheap, it was also very strong, leading to a great deal of drunkenness. Title of Drawing, "Very Fou."

*Show Jamie* — In writing this poem, I was misled by the image, thinking it was of a little boy with something in his eye. Show Jamie, in fact was a showman, who exhibited scientific specimens in jars. Title of Drawing, same as poem.

*Mr. and Mrs. Anderson* — I am not the first writer to find that this image recalls the Burns song, *John Anderson, My Jo, John*. Sir Thomas Dick Lauder made a similar connection in his introduction to Geikie's collected edition. Title of Drawing, "The Auld Couple."

*Soutar Johnny* — Geikie seems to have felt a strong empathy with the poems of Robert Burns. This image and the next were inspired by Burns poems. Title of Drawing, "Tam o' Shanter and Soutar Johnnie."

*The Jolly Beggars* — Yet another inspiration from the poems of Robert Burns. Title of Drawing, same as poem.

*Hallow Fair* — This was a festive occasion that took place for many years every autumn in the Grassmarket. It was essentially a horse fair and was discontinued around the time of the First World War due to the arrival of motorised traffic. Title of Drawing, "Scene at the All Hallow Fair."

*Come to Mammy, Dearie* — Title of Drawing, same as poem.

*He's had plenty!* — Title of Drawing, "He's just gotten plenty for the day."

*Street Snab* — Before he embarked on his murderous activities with Hare, this was how William Burke earned his living. Comparing Geikie's drawing with other images of Burke, I am convinced that Geikie must have witnessed this. Title of Drawing, "Cobler and Customer."

*Orphan Laddies* — One the least appealing aspects of Victorian Edinburgh was the presence of a large number of street children. Geikie probably found this group in the vicinity of Calton Hill, where they tended to congregate. Title of Drawing, "'Boiling Potatoes."

*Blind Fiddler* — Title of Drawing, "The Blind Fiddler."

*Heard in the Cougait* — Johnnie Dowie was a celebrated Edinburgh publican, whose tavern was frequented with such literary luminaries as David Hume, Robert Burns and Sir Walter Scott. It was situated in Liberton Wynd and demolished prior to the building of George IV bridge. Title of Drawing, "The Cowgate at the foot of Libberton Wynd."

www.ingramcontent.com/pod-product-compliance
Lightning Source LLC
Chambersburg PA
CBHW060622070426
42449CB00042B/2471